D0793670

Sandra Markle

Finding Home

Illustrated by
Alan Marks

Charlesbridge

With love for my husband, Skip Jeffery—S. M.

For my mother, Florrie Marks—A. M.

Acknowledgments

Sandra Markle would like to thank Dr. William Andrew, veterinarian for Tidbinbilla Nature Reserve; David Davies, Raymond Terrace Rural Fire Brigade; Dr. William Ellis, senior research officer, Koala Study Program, University of Queensland, Australia; Audrey Koosman, director, National Animal Trust Fund; and Dr. Daniel Lunney, principal research scientist, Department of Environment and Conservation, New South Wales.
A special thank you to Skip Jeffery for his loving support throughout the creative process.

Text copyright © 2008 by Sandra Markle
Illustrations copyright © 2008 by Alan Marks
All rights reserved, including the right of reproduction in whole or in part in any form.
Charlesbridge and colophon are registered trademarks of Charlesbridge Publishing, Inc.

Published by Charlesbridge
85 Main Street
Watertown, MA 02472
(617) 926-0329
www.charlesbridge.com

Library of Congress Cataloging-in-Publication Data
Markle, Sandra.
   Finding home / Sandra Markle; illustrated by Alan Marks.
     p. cm.
   ISBN 978-1-58089-122-6 (reinforced for library use)
1. Koala—Australia—New South Wales—Anecdotes. 2. Koala—Habitat—Australia—New South Wales—Anecdotes. I. Marks, Alan,1957– II. Title.
QL737.M384M26 2008
599.2'5—dc22   2007001473

Printed in China
(hc) 10 9 8 7 6 5 4 3 2 1

Illustrations done in watercolor, pen, and pencil on Daler Bloxworth paper
Display type and text type set in Elroy and Fairfield
Color separations by Chroma Graphics, Singapore
Printed and bound by Jade Productions
Production supervision by Brian G. Walker
Designed by Susan Mallory Sherman

It's September.

Spring in New South Wales, Australia,
has just begun,
but there's a hot breeze
threading through the leaves.
It wakes the female koala
curled up in the tree.
She lifts her big, black nose
and sniffs.
The air smells of eucalyptus leaves
and smoke.

Her joey, a nine-month-old female
sleeping beside her,
wakes and tries to climb into her pouch.
But the joey has grown too big for this safe place.
Instead, she climbs onto her mother's back.
Kangaroos and wallabies thunder past their tree.
Possums scurry after them.
Overhead a colorful cloud of parrots
flaps away from the forest
and a sugar glider sails by, riding the smoky air.

The female koala flees, too.
But she can't run fast for long,
or fly,
or glide away.
So, built to climb, she bounds
up,
up,
up as high as she can go in the tree.
Her joey hangs on tight
to ride along.

Fire sweeps through the forest—
crackling,
snapping,
roaring.
Waves of flames roll over brush,
crawl up tree trunks,
and leap through the air,
eating every leaf they touch.
Higher still—
as high as the huddled koalas—
swirls the mud-black smoke.
And through this thick cloud
swarms of sparks
fly, land, and
sting.

The female koala is lucky.
This bushfire is not as fierce as some.
And she's in a tree a little ways beyond a firebreak,
an area kept clear of brush.
So before the bushfire reaches her,
it runs out of fuel and stops.
The female koala escapes
with a burned patch on her back
from a flaming clump of leaves.
Her joey, squeezed between her and the tree trunk,
is unharmed.

But only shadow-black skeletons remain
where koalas once dined
on a daily buffet of different kinds of eucalyptus trees,
such as swamp mahoganies and forest red gums.

Beyond the forest the land is unburned,
but there are few trees there.

That night
the female koala climbs down
with her joey on her back.
As she waddles across the moonlit grass,
the shadow bumping after her
seems to chase her away
from the burned ruins
of her home range.

A little farther on, the female koala
lifts her big, black nose and sniffs the air.
She needs to eat leaves,
but not just any kind will do.
So when her keen sense of smell doesn't detect
any promising scents,
she waddles on.

Hour after hour,
the female koala searches for a meal.
Sometimes, when the burden of carrying her big joey is too much,
she shakes her shoulders.
The joey slips off and tags along
until the female koala stops to sniff the air again.
Then the joey quickly climbs back on to hitch a ride.

Finally the female detects the scent of food.
She follows her nose along a dry streambed,
across a field,
under a fence,
and between tall houses.
At last she sees what she's been tracking—
a swamp mahogany tree.

The female koala hurries toward her meal.
But before she can reach it, a shadow leaps to life,
running on four legs,
flashing white teeth,
and barking.
The moonlight reveals it's a
dog.

The female koala grunts,
kicks her screaming joey off,
and bounds away in rabbit-fast hops.
The dog chases after her,
snarling and growling.
When the dog gets close,
the female koala flops onto her back,
hissing,
with her razor-sharp claws
ready to scratch.

A loud shout from across the yard
makes the dog stop.
At a second shout, the dog gives one last growl
and trots away.
The female koala rolls to her feet
as a girl walks up and grabs the dog's collar.
For a minute, maybe longer,
the female koala and the girl stare at each other.
Koalas are native to Australia,
but they're rarely seen outside the bush.
So both the koala and the girl are curious about each other.

When the joey climbs onto her mother's back,
the girl takes the dog into the house.
Then the female koala climbs
up,
up,
up to the high, tender branches of the swamp mahogany.
There she snags a twig with her claw-tipped toes
and bites off just one leaf.
To digest the tough leaves, she has to chew them,
one at a time,
into little bits.

Her joey climbs onto the limb
to grab a leaf for herself.
But she keeps a tight grip on her perch
and her big nose bumps most of the leaves out of reach.
So after just a few nibbles, the joey returns,
pokes her head into her mother's pouch, and nurses.
Then she curls up to nap
while the female koala chews,
and chews,
and chews.

The sky is rosy and the air is already warming up
by the time the female koala climbs down
with her joey on her back.
In her home range she dined on several trees each night.
But, having come so far to find this one swamp mahogany,
she stayed to eat her fill—
nearly half a pound of leaves.
Now, she plods from yard to yard
searching for a bushier tree
to shade her from the day's bright heat.

Half a pound is just over 200 grams

She finds an acacia tree.
And high up in its branches, the female koala sleeps,
with her joey at her side,
until noises wake her.
Looking down through leaves and shadows,
she spies people
staring up at her.
She watches them between naps.
Each time she wakes, jolted by fresh bursts of noise,
the crowd she sees is bigger.

That night the female koala, with her joey on her back,
searches for another meal.
It is her habit to move to a different part of her home range
each night before settling down to eat.
So once again, she sniffs and hunts
from yard to yard
to find just one tree that is right.
But this time, as she waddles along, people trail after her.
More come later while she's eating,
and sometimes there are bright beams of light
that make her blink and her joey squeal.

For two more days, the koala moves from tree to tree.
In between eating and sleeping,
she watches and listens to the chattering, humming,
buzzing people that are always close by.
By the third night the crowd is so large
the female koala stays put longer than usual.
Then a warm wind flutters through the leaves.
It smells of dirt, green grass, people, and—
eucalyptus trees.
The female koala sets off,
tracking the scent of the trees.

The crowd tags along between houses,
through a gate,
along the side of a pond,
and across a field
to a large, black road.

The road is packed with parked cars and trucks
and people.
They are all stopped to let the koalas cross safely.
But there are still loud noises
and bright streaks of light.
The female koala stops at the edge of the road,
and her joey squeals.

Then after a bit,
one by one, the lights go out
and the noises stop.

Finally, the only light is moonlight.
The only sound is the wind,
carrying the scent of eucalyptus trees.
And the female koala, with her joey on her back,
follows her nose between the quiet walls of people
and across the large, black road.

Then she hurries into the forest and bounds up
to the high, tender branches of a forest red gum.

Behind her, noises and lights shatter the night again,
but the female koala pays no attention.
She's already chewing a leaf
and sniffing the many scents of her new home range.
Nearby her joey climbs onto a tree limb of her own,
reaches out to snag a leaf,
and starts to chew.

Author's Note

This story is based on the real-life story of a koala nicknamed Cinders that survived two bushfires. The first fire left her a serious burn victim, requiring special care for eleven months. After she recovered, Cinders was returned to the wild wearing a radio collar so researchers could keep track of her and be sure she could survive on her own in the wild. Less than a year later, a bushfire struck Cinders's new home range. This time, a firebreak saved her, but most of her feeding trees were destroyed. Researchers were surprised when Cinders walked an amazing twelve miles (twenty kilometers) in search of a new home. Cinders's journey became news when she crossed a busy highway and visited a suburb. She even spent a couple days visiting a Royal Australian Air Force Base. When Cinders settled into a new forested area, the radio collar was removed. She lived there for the rest of her life. Cinders's descendants are believed to still live in the forest home she adopted.

Koalas Are Amazing!

- The leaves of eucalyptus trees, such as swamp mahoganies and forest red gums, contain chemicals that would poison many other animals, but koalas are able to digest them safely because of special bacteria inside their bodies.
- After being born, a baby koala, called a joey, develops inside its mother's pouch for about six months. Then the joey stays with its mother another six months—sometimes longer—before it's ready to go off on its own.

For more information check out the following:

Australian Koala Foundation
   www.savethekoala.com/koalas.html
   Find out facts about koalas, see koala photos, and discover how you could foster a koala or help plant trees koalas need to eat.

Foundation for National Parks & Wildlife
   www.fnpw.com.au/enews3/bushfireKoalas.htm
   Read about the fires and koalas that provided the inspiration for *Finding Home*. Also learn about the foundation that supported the study of these koalas.

Kalman, Bobbie and Heather Levigne. *The Life Cycle of a Koala*. New York: Crabtree Publishing Company, 2002. An easy-to-read introduction to koalas that also explains how joeys develop inside a pouch.

Lang, Aubrey. *Baby Koala*. Ontario: Fitzhenry & Whiteside Limited, 2003. Photos by respected wildlife photographer Wayne Lynch illustrate the story of a baby koala's first year.